Before Using...

 A therapist's guide is enclosed loose with this book and should be removed and consulted before use.

To prevent bleed-through, it is recommended that water-based, rather than spirit-based, markers or pens be used in this Workbook.

A Separation in My Family

A Hunter House Growth and Recovery Workbook
by Wendy Deaton, M.A., M.F.C.C.
Series consultant: Kendall Johnson, Ph.D.
Illustrated by Cecilia Bowman

ISBN 0-89793-151-3

Ordering Information

Additional copies of this and other Growth and Recovery Workbooks may be obtained from Hunter House. Bulk discounts are available for professional offices and recognized organizations.

All single workbooks: $9.95   10-pack: $70.00
Workbook Library Special
(one of each workbook—10 total): $75.00

The Growth and Recovery Workbooks (GROW) Series

A creative, child-friendly program designed for use with elementary-school children, filled with original exercises to foster healing, self-understanding, and optimal growth.

Workbooks for children ages 9–12 include:

No More Hurt—provides a safe place for children who have been physically or sexually abused to explore and share their feelings

Living with My Family—helps children traumatized by domestic violence and family fights to identify and express their fears

Someone I Love Died—for children who have lost a loved one and who are dealing with grief, loss, and helplessness

A Separation in My Family—for children whose parents are separating or have already separated or divorced

Drinking and Drugs in My Family—for children who have family members who engage in regular alcohol and substance abuse

I Am a Survivor—for children who have survived an accident or fire, or a natural disaster such as a flood, hurricane, or earthquake

I Saw It Happen—for children who have witnessed a traumatic event such as a shooting at school, a frightening accident, or other violence

Workbooks for children ages 6–10 include:

My Own Thoughts and Feelings (for Girls); My Own Thoughts and Feelings (for Boys)—for exploring suspected trauma and early symptoms of depression, low self-esteem, family conflict, maladjustment, and nonspecific dysfunction

My Own Thoughts on Stopping the Hurt—for exploring suspected trauma and communicating with young children who may have suffered physical or sexual abuse

We welcome suggestions for new and needed workbooks

You are SPECIAL.

Write your name here
in a special way
that you like.

This is your book. In it
you can tell about how
your family has changed.

1

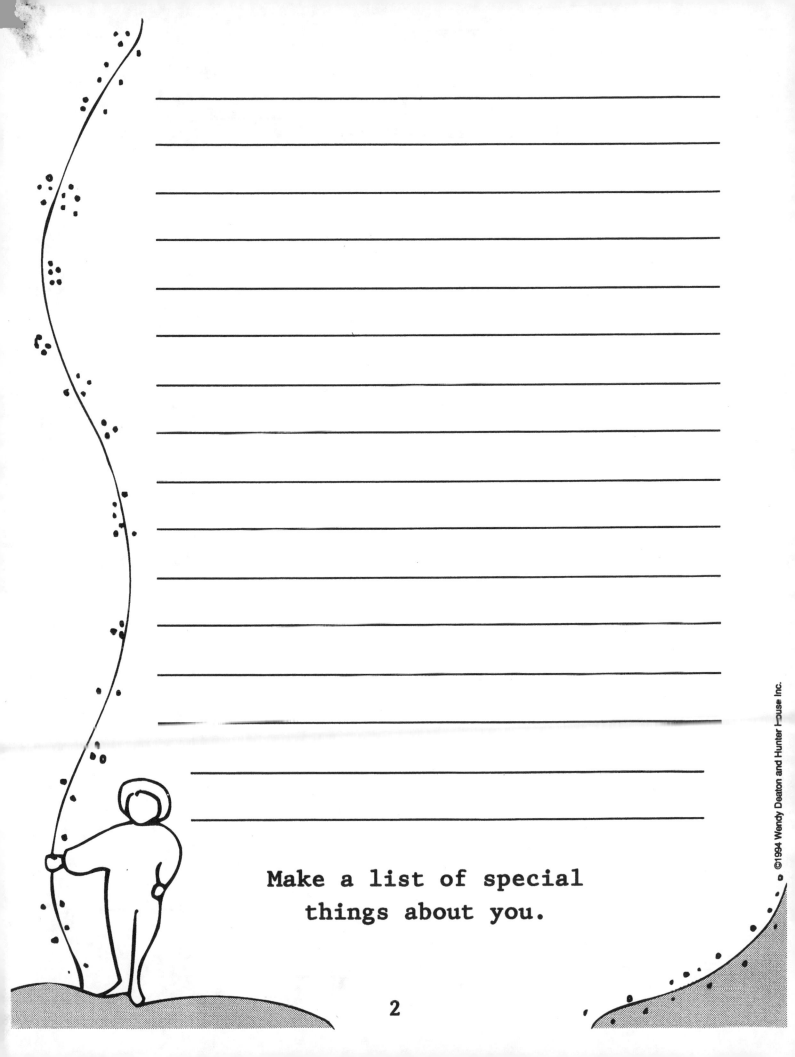

_____

_____

_____

_____

_____

_____

_____

_____

_____

_____

_____

_____

_____

_____

Make a list of special
things about you.

Draw a picture of how you feel today.

The word family can mean many things:

It can mean just the people who live in your house. It can mean all your aunts, uncles, cousins, and other "relatives." It can mean a group of people who have something they share. Or it can mean all the people you love and want to call your family.

What does family mean to you?

Here are some people who can be in your family:

- mothers
- nieces
- adopted parents
- stepmothers
- nephews
- your dog
- fathers
- aunts
- your cat
- stepfathers
- uncles
- special friends
- halfsisters

- cousins
- stepsisters
- stepbrothers
- godparents
- halfbrothers
- grandparents
- brothers-in-law
- dad's girlfriend
- foster parents
- sisters-in-law
- mom's boyfriend

Check anyone who is in your
family and add anyone else you
want in your family here:

_____

_____

_____

_____

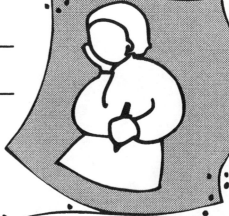

Something important has happened in your family. It is called a separation or divorce. Your mom and dad don't live together anymore.

This book is to help you understand what happened so that your life can go on...and be good.

What are all the reasons you think of why this separation or divorce has happened in your family?

_____

_____

_____

_____

_____

_____

_____

_____

_____

_____

_____

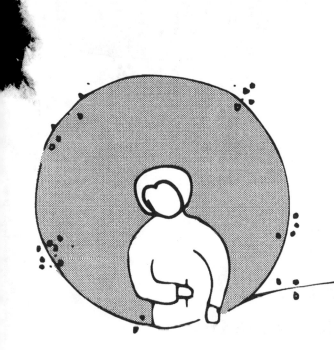

We all have many kinds of feelings. Some feelings feel good, like love, excitement, happiness. Some feelings feel bad, like fear, anger, and sadness.

There is no right or wrong about feelings.

There is no good or bad about feelings.

Feelings are just something that happen to you.

Everything you feel is okay.

What are some of your feelings about what happened in your family?

- sad
- glad
- like crying
- bad
- mean
- like laughing
- shy
- happy
- like screaming
- silly

- hurt
- like kicking
- mad
- sorry
- embarrassed
- guilty
- like hitting

Other feelings:

_____

_____

_____

_____

Draw a picture of your family
before the separation or divorce.

**Draw a picture of your family
after the separation or divorce.**

Do you ever think the separation or divorce is your fault?

Do you sometimes think something you did or something about you caused it to happen?

Do you ever think about how you can stop it from happening?

Write about your thoughts here:

_____

_____

_____

_____

_____

_____

_____

_____

_____

The separation or divorce was not your fault. You did not cause it and you cannot stop it.

The divorce was a decision your mom and dad made because they think it is the best decision for everybody.

It is not your decision, it is not your fault.

When Mom and Dad separate it changes many things. Some changes feel scary or sad and you won't like them. Like moving away from your friends or not having your Dad kiss you goodnight every night.

Some changes feel good or at least feel better. Like not having to listen to Mom and Dad fight every day.

Maybe now when you are with your mom or dad, you can have them all to yourself.

Have you talked with anyone about these changes?

Who would you like to talk with?

_____

_____

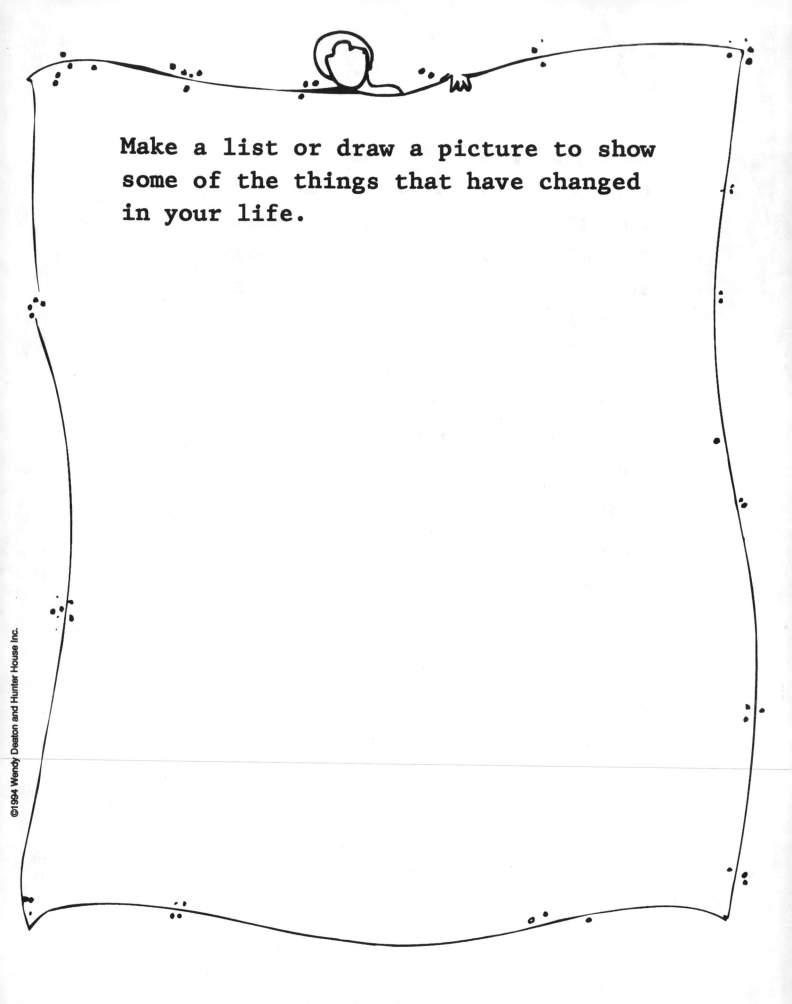

Make a list or draw a picture to show
some of the things that have changed
in your life.

Did you ever have a hard decision to make?

Did you ever have to choose between two things you really wanted?

Did you ever have to do something you didn't want to do because it was the "right" thing to do?

Did you ever do something that made you happy but other people unhappy?

Write about or draw a picture to show how it feels to make a hard decision.

The divorce or separation was a hard decision for your parents. They knew it would make some people unhappy. Sometimes you have to make a decision that other people don't understand or that makes some other people unhappy.

Draw a picture of how you think your parents felt when they made the hard decision to separate or divorce.

Do you have any "secret" feelings about the separation or divorce? Feelings that you have not told anyone about because you thought the feelings were bad or mean?

Any feelings you have about the divorce are okay. Your feelings are not bad. They are the same feelings other kids have had when their parents got divorced.

Write some of your "secret" feelings here, or draw a picture to show how the feelings feel.

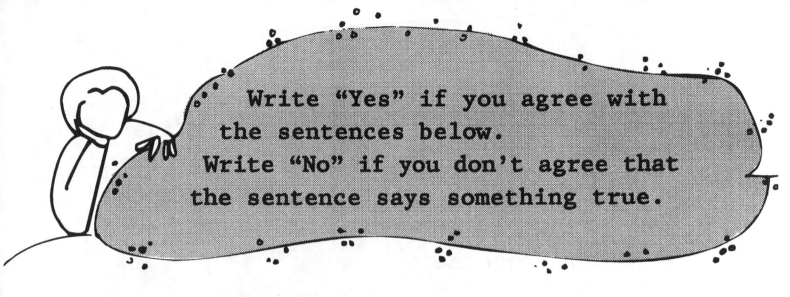

Write "Yes" if you agree with the sentences below.
Write "No" if you don't agree that the sentence says something true.

- Love lasts forever _____

- Love goes away _____

- Sometimes it hurts when you love somebody _____

- The more people you love, the more love you have _____

- Love happens only once in a lifetime _____

- Love keeps on growing _____

- There are lots of kinds of love _____

- Love makes you jealous _____

- You are not selfish with someone you love _____

- Love makes you sad _____

- Love makes you happy _____

Many things change when parents separate or get divorced. Some things don't change. Some things stay the way they have always been. Make a list of things that are the same now as when your family lived all together.

Have your counselor tell a story and you can draw the pictures here. Or write a story and draw pictures using one of these titles:

- ❧ The Little Prince/Princess
- ❧ Mom's House and Dad's House
- ❧ The Nightmare
- ❧ When Wishes Come True

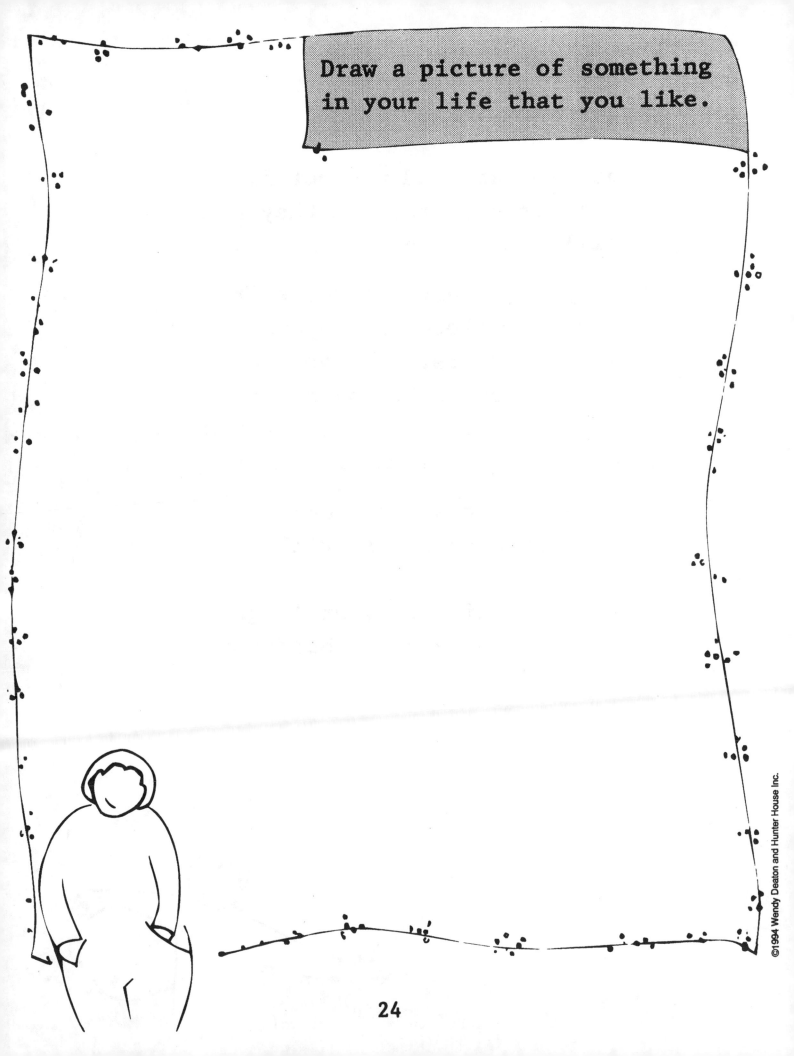

Draw a picture of something in your life that you like.

Your mom and dad may not live together anymore, but they are still your parents.

Everything that was yours from your mom before the separation is still yours. Like your hair is the same as her hair, or your eyes are the same, or you have the same sense of humor.

Everything that was yours from your dad before, is still yours. Like maybe your smile is just like his, or your laugh is the same, or you are both good in Math.

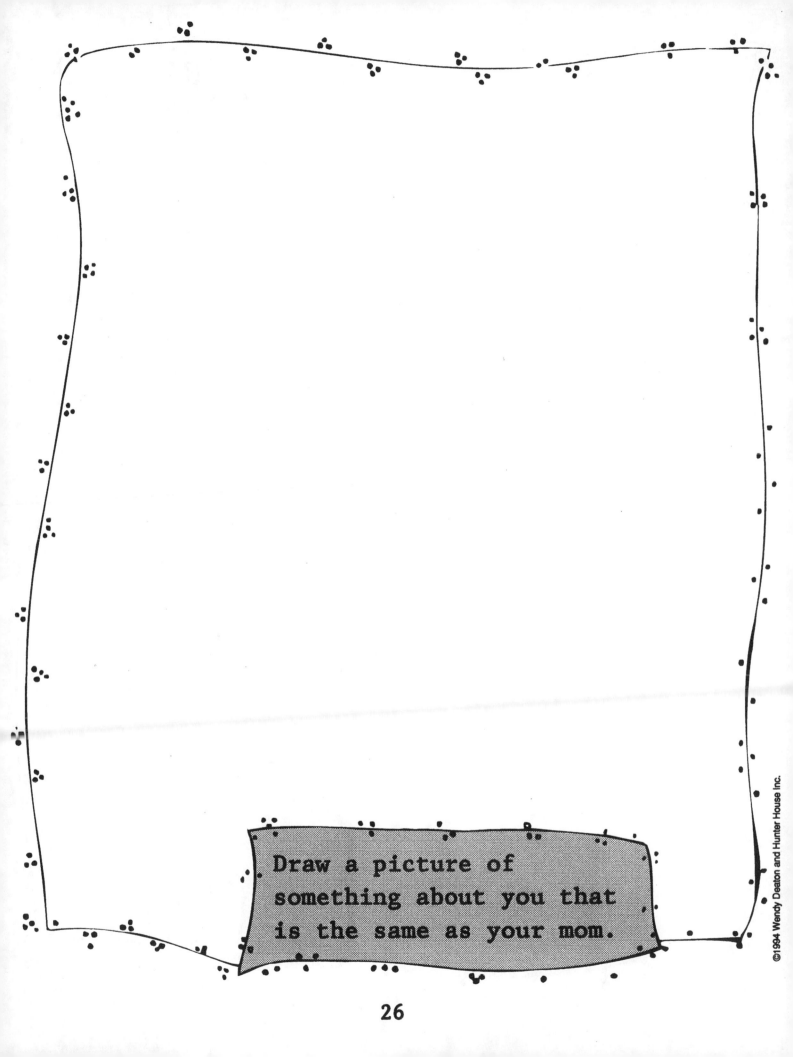

Draw a picture of
something about you that
is the same as your mom.

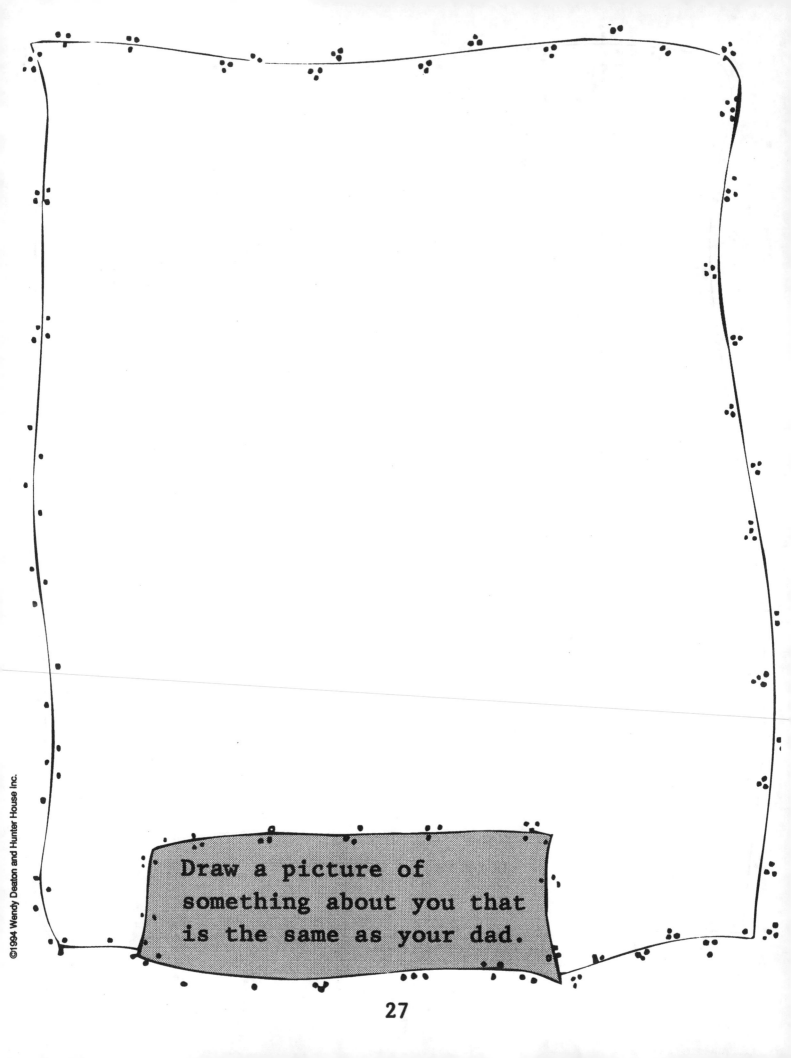

Draw a picture of
something about you that
is the same as your dad.

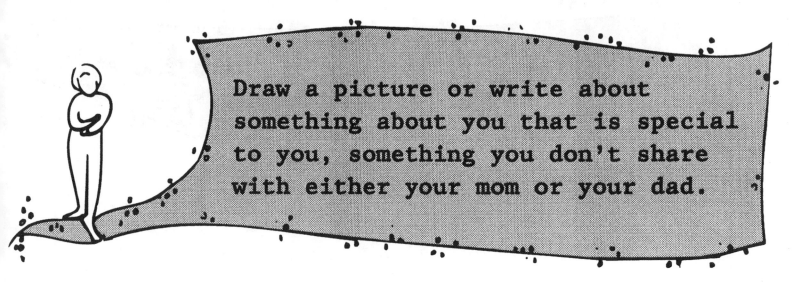

Draw a picture or write about something about you that is special to you, something you don't share with either your mom or your dad.

Write and draw a story with the title "My Favorite Family."

Draw a picture of your favorite
memory of your family.
No one can take this memory away.
It is yours forever.

Make three wishes for your family.

Draw a picture of you with all the people you love.

PLEASE READ THIS...

This is a brief guide to the design and use of the Growth and Recovery (GROW) workbooks from Hunter House. It is excerpted from detailed guidelines that can be downloaded from www .hunterhouse.com or are available free through the mail by calling the ordering number at the bottom of the page. Please consult the detailed guidelines before using this workbook for the first time.

GROW workbooks provide a way to open up communication with children who are not able to or who are reluctant to talk about a traumatic experience. They are not self-help books and are not designed for guardians or parents to use on their own with children. They address sensitive issues, and a child's recovery and healing require the safety, structured approach, and insight provided by a trained professional.

Each therapist will bring her own originality, creativity, and experience to the interaction and may adapt the tasks and activities in the workbooks, using other materials and activities. With less verbally oriented children, the use of art therapy or music or video may be recommended, or certain exercises may be conducted in groups.

Each pair of facing pages in the workbook provides the focus for a therapeutic "movement" that may take up one session. However, more than one movement can be made in a single session or several sessions may be devoted to a single movement. Children should be allowed to move through the process at their own pace. If a child finds a task too "hot" to approach, the therapist can return to it later. When something is fruitful it can be pursued with extended tasks.

While a therapist is free to select the order of activities for each child, the exercises are laid out in a progression based on the principles of critical incident stress management:

- initial exercises focus on building the therapeutic alliance
- the child is then led to relate an overview of the experience
- this is deepened by a "sensory-unpacking" designed to access and recover traumatic memories
- family experiences and changed living conditions, if any, are explored
- emotions are encouraged, explored, and validated.
- delayed reactions are dealt with, and resources are explored.
- the experience is integrated into the child's life through a series of strength-building exercises.

Specific pages in the GROW workbooks are cross-referenced to Dr. Kendall Johnson's book *Trauma in the Lives of Children* (Hunter House, Alameda, 1998). This provides additional information on the treatment of traumatized children.

The content of the workbooks should be shared with parents or significant adults only when the child feels ready for it and if it is therapeutically wise. Workbooks should not be given to children to take home until the therapeutic process is completed according to the therapist's satisfaction.

Although this series of workbooks was written for school-age children, the tasks are adaptable for use with younger children and adolescents.

Detailed guidelines are available for each GROW workbook (see list on front inside cover).